Ways of Healing
Charlotte Shevchenko Knight

NEW**POETS**LIST

the poetry business

Published 2022 by
New Poets List
An imprint of The Poetry Business
Campo House,
54 Campo Lane,
Sheffield S1 2EG

ISBN 978-1-914914-26-3
eBook ISBN 978-1-914914-27-0
Typeset by The Poetry Business
Printed by Biddles, Sheffield

Smith|Doorstop Books are a member of Inpress:
www.inpressbooks.co.uk

Distributed by IPS UK, 1 Deltic Avenue,
Rooksley, Milton Keynes MK13 8LD

The Poetry Business gratefully acknowledges the support
of Arts Council England.

Supported using public funding by
**ARTS COUNCIL
ENGLAND**
LOTTERY FUNDED

Contents

Moondaddy

Today the doctor asked if I was planning on
keeping it   Right now it is a grainy little moon
distorted by dark waves that I know

with the slightest change of tide
might pull us closer together   Being in love is like

drowning in space oh baby   you gaslight me so hard

The days when you pretend we do not know each other
fill me with all this understanding
for foxes   screaming in the night for want of sex   Imagine

your reaction to something concrete
proof of a world in which we have both existed
momentarily   even if it is just this

this malformed pearl   ready to be crushed

Mother of Pearl

My female relatives are thrilled I have been
impregnated by the sea. My belly a swollen pearl

they take turns stroking. At night, the pearl glows ochre.
I don't get much sleep. My aunties assure me this

is a good sign. My boss is not so impressed by my pearl
& I. We keep bumping into co-workers, making hollow

sounds. My pearl glows in annoyance. My co-workers
tell HR. I am asked to take parental leave at once.

I keep a dream journal to monitor my progress.
I write, whale song, saltwater, grain of sand, oyster knife.

My aunties pass it around in a circle, reading it like scripture.
My pearl grows stronger, glows holy, from their worship.

My maternity package is not very generous. It glows
like my cheeks, keeping me up at night. I am getting

even less sleep than before. Citizens Advice assure me
this is a good sign. *I am getting even less sleep than before,*

I tell the sea. The tide swells against my ankles
in a gesture of comfort. My pearl glows the colour

of an old coin. *Can you help us?* I ask. The water pulls away.
I lie with the windows open at night, listening out for the sea,

hoping child support will wash up on the shore, in waves
that clink with loose change. My pearl is less convinced

by this logic. Her light suddenly goes out.

Clinic / The Winter Self

i

Running into the sea fully-clothed is a symptom.
So are the crowds forming, the perpetual sunsets
& sharp applause. I am sick with wanting.

I just want to hold a child in the snow.
I want to dab their face with antibacterial wipes.

ii

After my January swim, which was more
a thrashing in the waves, lost in television static,
I buy a coffee made the wrong way, milk first.

Wet silk, beige gossamer, twirling around a cup.
I think back to the clinic, paper cups atop
a water cooler bubbling with mild anger.

I just want an answer: Is depression a glitter?
Does my empty womb mean something?

iii

I was born in January. My mother was afraid
to take me outside, for fear I would inhale cold air
& freeze from the inside out.

I picture my childhood self as a small instrument
made of glass into which air & spit is blown.

It produces an awful whistling which can only
be heard by dogs.

I am afraid of the sounds I make, the ways in which
my body alienates others.
I am afraid of the ceaseless winter of myself.

Someone lit a candle once

                                         & they died.
Some say of asphyxiation. Others, carelessness.
When I think of you I forget myself, forget my tongue,
how to taste. Garlic means nothing, & love is one big
conspiracy. The government is occupying my heart
while I sleep, stealing its pigeons, replacing their batteries.
It's a systemic ablation. I have woken to an FBI agent
hovering over me, scalpel in hand. I have asked, *hey,*
what are you doing? He has said, *I better call my lawyer.*
Love is one big super-injunction & I am backtracking,
I am forgetting the nasty things you have said, forgetting
the knife. There will be a sudden taste of rhubarb
before I remember I have forgotten how to taste.
Someone lit a candle once & the candle said *hey,*
what are you doing? & then they died. Some say of shock.
Others, cytokinesis, which is the physical process of cell division,
in which the cytoplasm of a parental cell divides into two daughters,
which is not what love is. I bear you no daughters.
I am wearing my shades as I walk into the clinic.
I am holding a state-issued flashing device which helps us to forget
that asteroids are falling on Mars right now, or that our daughter
is the size of a grape, or that she will never be anything more.

You are a Woman Marked for Sorrow

after Anne Carson's translation of Sophocles

for blood in silk underwear abdominal pains
clinic visits the uncaring doctor the uncaring
boyfriend the uber home in silence leftover
noodle grease on the sideboard chafed thighs
small messes sirens in the night hushed phone
calls in the hallway essential oils to lull you
to sleep lavender head chamomile pillow the man
who snores effortlessly next to you pelvic twinges
the sighing dog yearning to either have or become
a child cold cups of tea general forgetfulness care
at the centre of all your longing self-help books
crystal healing jade eggs swimming at dawn drinking
saltwater taking in all of nature wanting to become
a natural woman child-bearing hips fallopian hurries
questioning relatives & sorrow & sorrow & sorrow

Singing Before I Drown in a River in Denmark

mermaid-like & incapable
of my own distress i collect
    flora from the riverbank
        looting a natural ecosystem
    hoping to one day be framed
            in gold
       i carry my losses with me
    every flower a symbol
       how foxgloves are death
  how cattails   innocence
how pansies are love
         in vain
how you   you held me
    always obscured
in dark corners
       like with nature
    how easy to say
      we are separated
   tall grass
      wildflowers
  no waves
      no waves
a tributary husband
  we were subject
  to bursting banks
     breaking boughs
       overseas
    mad with grief
  singing for you
    till my muddy death

Insert Sappho Reference

pour wine over this white goat
or like hunt me for sport   oh baby
love a long fusillade of mistakes
burning holes in my new purple furs
love a frenetic chasing why do i have
four legs   or love a fecund horn sounding
& me & my pheromones   so very
tangible   you can smell them
in the cheese   like the things you awoke
in me   your head a bunch of violets
my lap a goat's lap can i collect this
as a sadness can i carry this hurt
in a basket specifically woven
for the occasion   can i be exiled
is there an island for heartbroken
goats why am i bleating when i say
[insert sappho reference] i mean i get it
we have all loved somebody
with the knowledge that they won't
love us back i mean i don't get it
i am a goat   why am i crying

Apollonia Ponders

What if we kissed
          & all my teeth fell into your mouth
What if we kissed
& the kiss was pink liquid,
            was a rosewater
What if stuffed vine leaves
we pass between mouths
         What if goat's milk
What if I was of notable
Christian faith
   or lived
on a golden island
What if teeth = rejection
      & every dream has a meaning
What if every poem
    was a pink liquid
& when we kissed
our tongues became petals
What if soft   island `
    a saintly presence
What if we jumped into the fire
      & you a husband
What if we forged this
    What if we invoked each other
         for toothache
           for some other pain

Folklore

today the weather is holding
like an apple   & sunlight touches moss
in a blurry way   as if behind a screen
if you turn your television on   the latest news
is that i have fallen in love with you
while walking through the forest a sharp feeling
like putting a coin in your mouth
that tastes unlucky   it happened
the moment a branch snapped
beneath my wellies   & i gasped
thinking it was the sound of a wish-
bone breaking   the wish was yours
the trees were bent with golden
yearning   a pit opened in the ground
& i fell down   willingly

Shotgun

in casual circumstance we met
orange slices floating in beer
to flirt with a stranger steal
his hat   the decision was drunken
& therefore superficial
i liked yr crooked nose   u thought
my face was blue   & moon-like
the pub was outside a church
our friends were already
present at least physically
our spirits

       in the astral plane
       above the spires
       star-dependent
       oblivious
to calculate the age of a tree
count its rings   u proposed
on a saturnalia   to predict
the future

       buy me a drink
       inside we wrote invites
on the backs of coasters
slid them over to men
mindlessly playing snooker
we scampered

         to the graveyard
      excited bunnies
our guests   old voyeurs
my veil made of napkins
yr nerves   gunmetal

our vows   holy babbles
to have found   a love
as rare   as the smoke
of a shotgun   to hunt
the moon   like a rabbit
                or a mock sun

We're Having Sex in a Dorset Forest

& i'm cumming over lilypads!

if i had asked for sex to be sorrowful ...

for a body wrapped in vine leaves

tossed in a river & carried off ...

(crushed eggshells beneath my shoes

a disapproving bluebird's song)

if i had asked to be made shiny!

shakespearean nymph

glistening pond

asked you to drink of me

remember what I taste of ...

if i had asked for cheeks to blush

red with iron

like a sexy marmalade ...

like the colour of dusk ...

& white harts everywhere ...

white harts EVERYWHERE!

daisies in the wind all watching us ...

Poem That Ends with a Baby

a micro pig is set loose in the yard & i have
no husband to help me. it is raining. the pig
is running mascara i am wearing a white dress
you can see my nipples & my breasts bounce
the dress is polluted by sky-stains now thanks
a lot weather. i can hear the neighbour complain
the squealing she thinks i am having sex & yes
i do often make that sort of noise unholy opera
but really not in this weather & i want to explain
that to gail knock on her door offer cinnamon bun
& half-hearted apology but there is no time. i must
gather up this micro pig. & when i gather up this
micro pig i will cradle it to my chest like a dirty
baby, which is exactly what it is.

I Want to Swallow a Lightbulb

It's my birthday & I'm breaking the law
by touching your hand at the beach.

I'm supposed to lie down in the sand with you.
I'm supposed to let crabs crawl over my body

& get jealous when they start crawling over yours.
This year let's not say mean things

to each other. Everyone else is free game though.
My neighbour runs from me like a muntjac,

failing to understand that we are all angry at someone;
the way the sun courses closer to our planet is proof of that.

After promising not to write about you anymore
I spent three long days wondering how I'd feel

if God took the ocean away from us.
I still haven't decided.

The Abduction of Air

Because God didn't make us aviary creatures,
& the sky won't work the way we want it to,

I set an alarm for when the weatherman
claims there will be snow. I am trying to prove

humanity wrong. I have a great disdain
for aeroplanes, the human presumption

of flight. When the Met Office send a super-
computer into the atmosphere & let its wings

scrape humidity into wet clouds, like remnants
of gelato in a metallic tub, that's a bit perverted.

Call it data capture, call it the abduction of air.
Lately, every house I visit has a power cut. The joke

being I'm unwelcome. Perhaps domesticity senses
my allegiance to the wild, & is resisting me

through broken lightbulbs. If a wasp buries itself
in a fig, & you take a bite, unaware, & the wasp

stings your throat, depriving you of wider air,
that's nature's revenge. Die on swollen note.

Iris Behind Glass

Iris is a half-formed face, severed from a body
whose thick neck suggests would have been stout.

I imagine Iris fully-formed, body simply not yet
visible, swimming in a pool of oil, rainbowing

around her head a slick halo. Where her eyes
are void, I give Iris hagstones, their fertile properties

likely to grant her sight. I bribe her marble with wheat,
honey & dried figs, whispering *I know who you are.*

Iris, behind glass, tell us what you see: an abandoned
chapel, overgrown with kindness — ivy leaves,

an accumulation of moss, deer flitting away
through a hidden door, a circle of women who worship

the malformed, who weave a corona of holly branches,
charred from the cold. Or a reflection of your half-face,

a menagerie of tourists. In the distance, an exit sign,
glimmering for your approval.

Mammal Fever

wending through the peat / under the new snow moon / no shoes
on my feet / i have come to commune / with ancient winds /
& barn owl whistles / with dry skin / against love-sharp thistles /
we are running out of time / in this chalk white forest /
i am running out of rhymes / to explain our solace / we are on earth
as particles / complacent with our blood / as peachy as cardinals /
courting amongst shrubs / embrace the mammal fever / that drives you
through the night / the sky is an unbeliever / we are running out of light

My Heart is Being Held Hostage by the World's Saddest Ending </3

after Sophie Robinson

by heart i mean four
chambers & blood
but also the accumulation
of memories allowing
you to still exist in my life:
your half-face on the jubilee
line to stratford
(a handsome moon
appropriately silver)
mumbling into an adidas
mask that you will
always [   ] me
an argument over
who will cook dinner
wooden spoon paddling
into the grotesqueness
of ass cheeks
when we came together
(even though it only
happened once)
& we stopped to marvel
as though witnessing
a sunset
for the last time
i will reassemble
your daily image
thru stolen sweatshirts
grizzly bear lyrics

caramel iced lattes
steam engines
heart emojis <3
magic seaweed
alarm bells
& a fear
of crowded places
& while there's a gun
pressed to my heart
i may as well admit
that you're the only one
to give me *endless poetry*
& *dancing dog* & that
i've never spent so much
time in either forest
sea or love x

Shame Sunday

is so violent katie says i have been hungover
many days my head feels like a child's dirty

hands grabbing at the fruit of a níspero tree
red juices running down their small wrists

the bells banging in the churchyard
i am famously incapable of processing

my emotions in a healthy way my friends
are becoming used to this they gather

around my body curled in its bed a king
prawn in paella forming a circle chanting

LIFE IS NOT A FEVER DREAM
CHARLOTTE WAKE UP

i sizzle in place eyes black & shining
try to form a thought like onyx that doesn't

revolve around the failures of my body
dig my nails into valencian sand

Durdle Doom

when i'm getting bad again flick drives us
to the rocks lets my body collapse into pebbles

& doesn't judge me when i cry remember
the summer a man climbed up the limestone

arch & flung himself into the purple horizon?
the way the crowd formed cheered for death

jurassic sunset when i get drunk i feel ancient
as in this is what poets do i am writing my body

into tradition my friends won't let me go into
the sea flick says i'll have forgotten how to float,

the salt won't carry me i've realised not a lot will
i want to be eroded watch the waves wink violently

whiskey soda but flick says we need to leave by 8pm
flick asks if i'm still taking my meds which friends

would gather my bones & which would feel relief
i wonder if i were to die on a national heritage site?

Ways of Healing

if yr dreams are plagued by mice hot lavender porridge
in the morning if a sinister haar settles over the village
if a child's cries are thick w/ illness rub unbroken eggs
& rosemary sprigs across their body wave an eagle's feather
any time u sense their fear for broken bones pass the child
thru a cleft in an ash sapling for a broken heart place rose
quartz beneath yr tongue grip yr mouth shut hope for the best
after a negative pregnancy test find a wet hill to roll down pout
yr lips whilst u roll kiss the ground as much as possible lie down
in a bush of milkweed let its pearly sap ooze over yr sunspots
in damage there is healing my mother recommends rubbing hot
vinegar across my breasts i'm not sure what for before a party
stuff yr bra w/ cabbage leaves for perkier nipples trust me
to draw blood from the earth bury a spoon in the garden a clover
will grow pluck it place it on yr tongue it should dissolve leaving
behind a metallic taste the morning after a breakup strip down
to yr underwear on a public beach walk into the winter waves
this is as close as u'll get to being vulnerable again

Acknowledgements

I'm grateful to the editors of *Lighthouse, Neutral Spaces, Outspoken Press* and *SPAM Zine*, in which some of these poems first appeared.

I'd like to thank the Poetry Society for their encouragement and support following the commendation of 'Moondaddy' in the National Poetry Competition.

Thank you to my teachers: Stephen Knight, Francis Spufford, Eva Salzman, and Richard Scott. A special thank you to Jack Underwood for his continuous kindness and mentorship over the years.

Thank you to my parents, Rick and Polina. To my sister, Ellamae. To my Goldsmiths cohort. To Scarlet Clark, Sidrah Zubair, Ruth Boon, Ella Sadie Guthrie and Katie O'Pray, my trusted readers. To my editor Suzannah Evans, judge Kim Moore and The Poetry Business, for granting me this opportunity. And to my loves. You know who you are.